MORE TRUTH THAN POETRY

by the same author

THE BALLAD OF THE SAD YOUNG MEN
AND OTHER VERSE

INVADE MY PRIVACY

MORE TRUTH THAN POETRY

Fran Landesman

JAY LANDESMAN LIMITED
LONDON

To Elton John
(Guess why)

First published in 1979 by
Jay Landesman Limited
159 Wardour Street
London W1

British Library Cataloging in Publication Data

Landesman, Fran
More Truth Than Poetry
I. Title
811'.5'4 PS3562.A47/

ISBN 0 905150 19 8

Printed in Great Britain by The Anchor Press Ltd
and bound by Wm Brendon & Son Ltd
both of Tiptree, Essex

CONTENTS

BIRD'S EYE VIEW

ROGUE'S GALLERY

Bird's Eye View

Deja Views, Australia

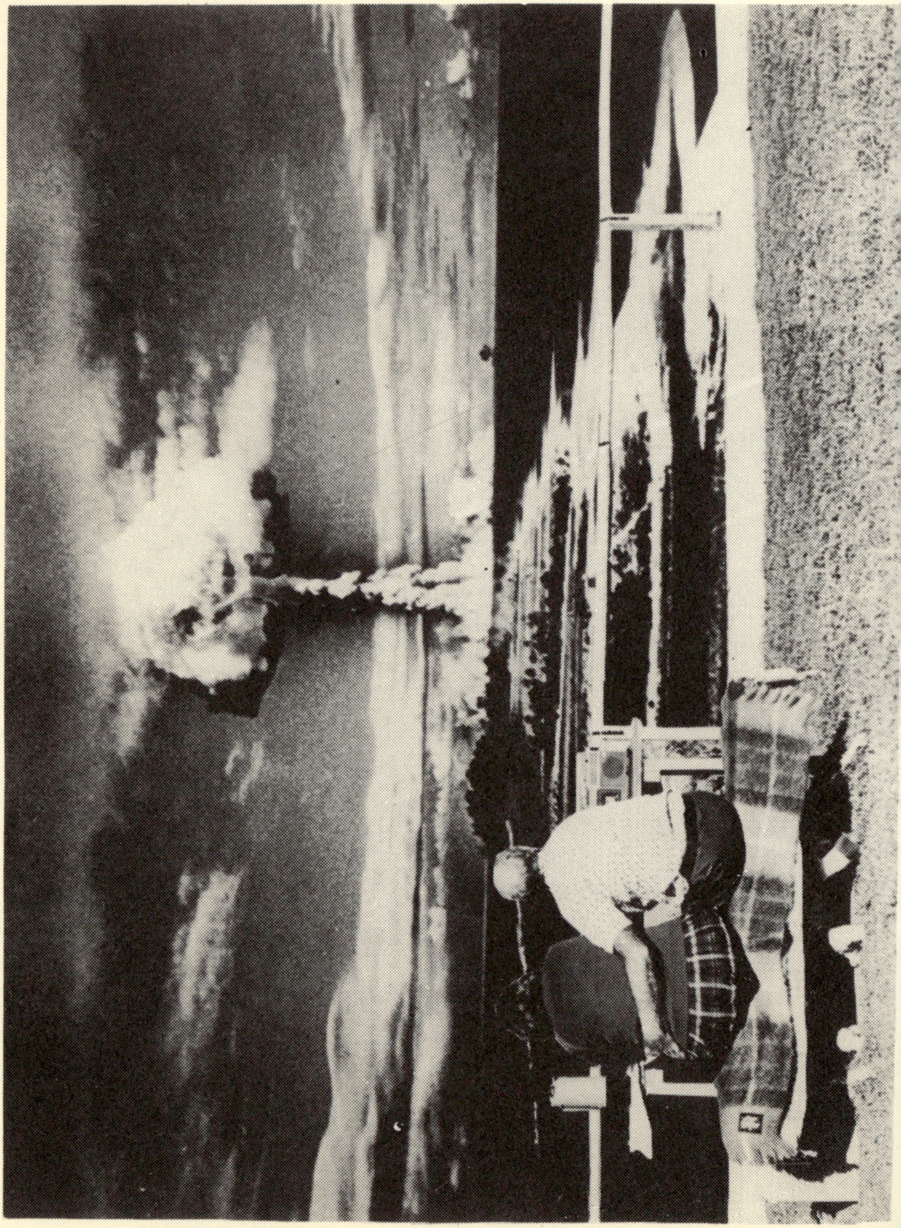

Bird's Eye View

From Dimity's Photograph

The old dears picnic on a tartan blanket
His hairy arm in short-sleeved sport shirt
Circumnavigates her waist
We see them from the rear
His balding head, her spreading bum
The edge of a carton of cholesterol
And a thermos of tea

Growing out of the horizon
Is the fabulous mushroom
Or is it the tree at the end of the world
With an angel in its branches?
(Do I see an angel?)
It is very beautiful and terrible to behold
But is it as awful as arthritis
Or the losing of a lover
Or the fear of growing old?

The Grooves of Change

Familiar faces alter
And familiar scenes grow strange
The great world keeps on spinning
Down the ringing grooves of change

The music of the sixties
Sounds sedate and sadly sweet
The records go on spinning
To an ever madder beat

The skyline goes on shifting
And old lovers disappear
The stars wear different faces
From the ones they wore last year

The punks are in the money
And the dollar's falling down
The peacock throne is empty
And John Lennon's out of town

The magazines turn yellow
In the rooms we used to haunt
And we don't know who to follow
And we don't know what we want

We muse about the future
And the jokes fate may arrange
As the great world keeps on spinning
Down the ringing grooves of change

Life Is a Bitch

Life is a bitch
From the cradle to the grave
Even when you're rich
You are always something's slave

Life is a bitch
Full of hang-ups, full of hurt
First love makes you itch
Then it dishes you the dirt

Just watch how the six-year-olds
Break each other's hearts
Better learn to stand the cold
Cultivate the arts

Life's full of shit
Even when you're in your prime
Though your show's a hit
Reason never seems to rhyme
Every joke has a switch
Every joker a twitch
Every high has a hitch
Baby, life is a bitch

Cigarettes

Man's inhumanity to man
Is the curse of the species we call human
A well accepted part of nature's plan
Is man's inhumanity to women

He told me he was goin' down to the corner
To get a pack of cigarettes
That happened in September now it's December
I haven't seen his shadow yet

Your man may be an angel, maybe you trust him
But I sure wouldn't take no bets
When he tells you that he's goin' down to the corner
To get a pack of cigarettes

It doesn't seem to matter if it's day or if it's night
A man will get distracted if you let him out of sight
So chain him to the bedpost, that's the only thing to do
If someone's gonna mess around it might as well be you

Of course men give good loving
They're often quite good looking
And some of them are little pets
But if you want to keep one
Don't get a deep one
And don't run out of cigarettes

The Bitter Joys of Vinegar

The other day there came to me
A thought both sad and funny
You'll catch more flies with vinegar
Than you can catch with honey

I've given you my heart and shirt
Some laughs and poems and money
But you prefer her vinegar
You don't care much for honey

"You'll catch no flies with vinegar"
My mother used to say
But it's been my experience
It works the other way

I've seen her order you about
I've watched her crucify you
If I were made of sterner stuff
I'd torment and deny you

Instead of which I dote on you
And try to make life sunny
The bitter joys of vinegar
Entice you more than honey

Bums Never Get Bald

Why does the Devil have all the best songs?
Why do the charmers just string you along?
Why are the goodies so boring as well?
How come they throw the best parties in hell?

The world is crowded with excellent types
I never could care for at all
The scrimpers and savers and smokers of pipes
Who won't ever stumble or fall

The rogues and rascals have radiant eyes
The work-all-day Daddies look grey
The scamps and scoundrels are sexy and wise
And gypsies are great in the hay

The sports and sinners though down on their luck
Don't run out of women and drink
The sane and sober are sure to get stuck
As life disappears down the sink

Chorus: And bums never get bald
They may sleep out in the cold
And go without dinner
And get a bit thinner
But bums never get bald

Make Lemonade

If you like the life you live it
If you've got the time you give it
If you see the chance you take it
If you want some bread you bake it
Turn off all those broadcasts that make you feel afraid
And if you've got lemons—make lemonade

If you've got a song you sing it
If you've got an axe you swing it
If you've got a horse you ride it
If you see the joke don't hide it
If you've got the muscle, go to your brother's aid
If you've got lemons—make lemonade

"Look at all the bummers" everybody says
Mankind's headin' for hell in a hurry
Radicals and slummers, acid heads and gays
Everyone's got his own brand of worry
"Baby, ain't it awful!" that's the game they play
But they ain't doin' nothin' about it
If their talk could fix it, that would be OK
But it can't so let's boogie on without it

If the records nowhere change it
If you want to you'll arrange it
If you like the life you live it
You can take or you can give it
Go ahead and do it—go out, get high, get laid
Or if you've got lemons
Make lemonade

The Code of the West

I'd much rather stay here with you in the evening
And read a good book while you cook me a stew
I don't want to go to the pub with my buddies
But a man's gotta do what a man's gotta do

I don't want to spend all those nights playing poker
With Fat Man and Joel and that whole feckless crew
It gets pretty dull watching football for hours
But a man's gotta do what a man's gotta do

You've seen westerns from Destry to Shane
And The Gunfight at OK Corral
And the message is written quite plain
You just gotta be true to your pals

A whole lot has changed since the days of the cowboys
The women get smarter but men are still men
And Saturday night brings the old obligation
A man's gotta do it and do it again

You know way down deep that I really do love you
Though I gotta chase any face that is new
I gits pretty weary sweet-talking those scrubbers
But a man's gotta do what a man's gotta do
Yes, a man's gotta do what a man's gotta do

The Game

The aim of the game
Is mainly in the pain
But it's so fascinating
The loving and the hating
The sighing and the praying
We've got to go on playing

The first few times it happened
We just couldn't work it out
But now we see the pattern
We know what it's all about

The aim of the game
Is mainly in the pain
A circle of frustration
Rejection and elation
Depression and obsession
A terrible connection

We're like compulsive gamblers
But our chips come from the heart
And we won't leave the table
Though the game tears us apart

The aim of the game
Is mainly in the pain
We're dizzy and despairing
But still we go on caring
Although the hurt keeps growing
Somehow it keeps us going
We've got to go on playing
The game

Song for Four Women
(The nun, the schoolgirl, the whore and the lion tamer)

Is this how you see us?
Is this how you want us to be?
Both virgin and hooker, attached to a cooker
Eternally youthful and free?

Is this how you see us
Is this how you'd like us to look
Erotically trashy, seductively flashy
Four girls from a hot picture book?

The nun provides the challenge
Forbidden fruit is sweet
The stripper's always ready
An eager bitch on heat
The lion tamer lures you
You long to kiss her feet
The schoolgirl makes you hunger
For tender, untouched meat

Is this how you'd have us?
Is this how you want us to act?
The perfect domestic, but enthusiastic
When you're in the mood to attack?

Is this what you're into
The smooth-talking satin-skinned tart
Who'll kiss you and hug you, too clever to bug you
With anything straight from the heart

Well isn't it a pity
That sometimes life intrudes
Into your Penthouse dream life
And please don't think us rude

If we're not always ready
To pose like Penthouse nudes
It seems that we've developed
Some other aptitudes

Is this what you wanted
When you were a small spotty boy
An all-giving mother for you and no other
Your very own pneumatic toy?

Is this how you see us
As ponies you train to do tricks
Or big-tittied bunnies? Well isn't that funny
We see you as bloodthirsty pricks!

One Man's Poison

One man's poison is another man's pie
One man's living lets another man die
One man's garden is another man's ditch
One man's baby is another man's bitch

Someone's future is another one's past
Someone's first love is another man's last
You get higher as your brother slips back
One man's heaven is another man's rack

One man's ideals are another man's dinner
You're getting fat while your brother gets thinner
It's a yin-yang world
With a sting in its tail
One collects the prize
As the next goes to jail

Some get angel cake all covered with jam
Friends keep telling me how lucky I am
But where is the playbox I left all my toys in?
One man's meat is another man's poison

So Says My Song

Why can't I write a happy song
With bluebirds singing all day long
Why do the storm clouds hide the sun
In all my songs

Why can't I sing of honey days
A song of joy, a song of praise
Why must I sing of all the ways
That love goes wrong

I may write a verse that is funny
But mostly laments are my thing
For somehow the song of the honey
Seems less than the song of the sting

Why can't I chant the positive
Because I find it hard to live
With all the hurts that love can give
So says my song

And earth is fair and flesh is fine
There's wine to share for Auld Lang Syne
But death is still the bottom line
So says my song

I Wrote the Part

I devote my life to making small jokes and screwing
And I spend my spare time polishing my art
And you ask me if I'm happy in what I'm doing
I ought to be—I wrote the part

Though behind the scenes my life isn't always pretty
And the smile I wear can't hide my battered heart
And a lot of friends will tell you that it's a pity
I can't complain—I wrote the part

I made my mind up when I was a kid
The way I wanted my story to be
I made the movie, the things that I did
All added up to the monster that's me

All the men I love go off to see other ladies
While I try to get a torch song in the charts
And I patronise the boozer next door to Hades
But what the hell—I wrote the part

Seems like everytime I get a real hit of gladness
It's not long before the complications start
But I've always liked my comedy laced with sadness
And that's the way
I wrote the part

Rogues Gallery

Rogues Gallery

Beautiful Ruin

She's a beautiful ruin
You can see the sky through her eyes
She's a flame that expires
With a gentle glow as it dies

She's a fabulous loser
You can see the sky through her eyes
And you long to believe her
While she keeps on telling you lies

Sometimes I feel the menace
She faces constantly
She makes me think of Venice
Slipping away into the sea

She's a flower that's fading
To a colour softer than Spring
She's a beautiful ruin
And she makes my heart want to sing

The Artist vs. Death

Now you live on morphine and oxygen
And you're fighting for your life
And you go making your twisted jokes
To the horror of your wife

Though the black magician is at the door
You resist him all the way
And he'll never get you to shut your eyes
While there's still a game to play

Don't you remember in St Louis summertime
All the broken treasures that we used to find
You taught me how to see
Your visions live in me
And I'll always hear you whisper in my mind

You're a combination of Georgie Raft
And a funny kind of saint
And it gives me the blues every time I think
Of the pictures you'll never paint

There are many others that I could spare
And it seems a bit obscene
That I sit in London and scribble verse
While you're living on morphine

Dream Girl

I've got me a dream girl
Peaches and cream girl
The kind you see on the cover of
A shiny magazine

I met a pretty model
And took her home one night
I couldn't wait to kiss her
She seemed to be Miss Right
But she removed her lashes
And then her golden hair
And when she stood there ticking
She gave me quite a scare

But she was a dream girl *etc*

I took her and shook her
I wasn't being rude
But I was really bothered
When both her arms unscrewed
So then I grew suspicious
I tore off both her tits
And found that I was holding
Two lovely counterfeits

I was losing my dream girl *etc*

Beneath her chest of plastic
A nest of wires lurked
I studied her transistor
And saw the way she worked
I put her back together
She sure was full of life
And if you're ever out our way
Come by and meet the wife

One of Them

In the kingdom of the freaks
The normal woman
Looms over her midget lover
Like a menace.
Hans flees from tiny Frieda
Breaking a faithful heart
For the masochistic gratification
Of giant thighs.

On Honeymoon
In 1950 when freaks were not so chic,
We flung ourselves on the A train
To find Tod Browning's masterpiece
Roosting briefly in Brooklyn.

Who can forget
The freaks assembled at the wedding supper?
They ring the table chanting
'We accept her one of us, one of us, one of us'
The normal woman shrieks in terror
And carries off her bridegroom like a child.

We stumbled out of the cinema
In search of egg creams
But the chicken woman had swallowed my appetite
I felt alone in the night
With the groom and his freaky friends
Wondering what bits of me might have to be
Chopped off
To make me one of them.

Why I'm Not Gay

She always used to tell me
"Some day you'll come around
When you get sick and tired
Of men who put you down."

She conquered men so lightly
From shipping clerk to sheik
Her beauty made them dizzy
Her courage made them weak

And I was always conquered
I always lost my heart
But never to a lady
Perhaps I wasn't smart

She never did convince me
Her arguments were sound
But I was still a sucker
For men who put me down

She hasn't lost her beauty
Her skin is still like cream
And though we keep our distance
I've met her in a dream

You'd think that I might risk it
If only for a thrill
But I'm too masochistic
And so I never will

I see her semi-yearly
When she flies through our town
I'm still not sick and tired
Of men who put me down

Caroline Coon

Caroline Coon, Caroline Coon
Does punk rock energy cause you to swoon
You're always in with the young and the brave
Riding the crest of the latest new wave

Don't we feel like we're supergirl
Putting punk in the charts
Aren't we having a super time
Putting down all the old farts

Caroline Coon, Caroline Coon
What are you taking that makes you immune
Everyone ages, their reflexes slow
You're still a swinger and still in the know

Aren't we having a lot of fun
Patronising the poor
Does it make us feel gratified
Sexy and secure

You're a vulture for teenage culture
And a journalistic whizz
What makes you think that music
Is just what you say it is

Caroline Coon, Caroline Coon
Some day you'll dry up like any old prune
Maybe I'm sore 'cause I know you'll dismiss
Old fashioned, middle class lyrics like this

Been Doin' Nothin'

In me you see no patriarch
Why go to work or take a wife?
I'm never going to leave a mark
Been doin' nothin' all my life

I haven't got one problem solved
I detour round the strains and strife
I just don't want to get involved
Been doin' nothin' all my life

Intoxication and hilarity
Loom large in my biography
Why should I care about posterity?
What has it ever done for me?

I haven't got a thing to hide
I do not own a fork or knife
Don't say I'm beat, I'm never tired
Been doin' nothin' all my life

The Death of the Lion Queen

The Lion Queen lies dying
Her children all have fled
Her saffron sheets need changing
Her cats have not been fed

Her house fills up with rubbish
Her hair has lost its shine
She bites her lips in anguish
And sips the dregs of wine

The Lion Queen is crying
The neighbours shut their ears
No more will she go hunting
Or taste the heroes' spears

She's eaten up with anger
Her flesh begins to stink
Her husband and her lover
Have gone out for a drink

The tricks time plays on beauty
Are subtle and obscene
But death will do his duty
And serve the Lion Queen

Love Lore

Love Lore

Semi-Detached

My sweetie and I are semi-detached
We're comfy and cool and perfectly matched
His lover is Ann. My lover is Art.
We're semi-detached but never apart

When some of our loves are semi-destroyed
We make it alright by quoting them Freud
We play little games and never get scratched
It's easy because we're semi-detached

Sometimes a playmate leaves us
For unconnected charms
But when a parting grieves us
We've got each other's arms

We each have a side that's free as the air
And people don't see the side that we share
Our set-up is sweet. There isn't a catch
The secret is living semi-detached

Depravity

Once you seemed much closer than my skin to me
We used to crawl inside your favourite symphony
And help each other hide out from reality
Now all we've got in common is depravity

I listened to your twisted brand of politics
Applauded when you did your famous parlour tricks
But now our long run fun affair is short of kicks
And all we've got in common is we need a fix

At first it was better than dreaming
Your hands and your lips made it real
I thought it was love we were making
But we were just making a deal

It's funny how we never seem to separate
Since both of us are dreaming of another mate
Two melancholy monkeys in captivity
And all we've got in common is depravity

Come With Me

Come with me, go with me, burn with me, glow with me
Write me a sonnet or two
Sleep with me, wake with me, give with me, take with me
Love me the way I love you

Let me get high with you, laugh with you, cry with you
Be with you when I am blue
Rest with you, fight with you, day with you, night with you
Love me whatever I do

Work with me, play with me, run with me, stay with me
Make me your partner in crime
Handle me, fondle me, cradle me tenderly
Say I'm your reason and rhyme

Pray with me, sin with me, lose with me, win with me
Love me with all of my scars
Rise with me, fall with me, hide from it all with me
Nothing is mine now, it's ours

The Failure of E.S.P.

If it were possible for a mind
To call another mind
You'd be here at my door
If I were master of E.S.P.
I'd bring you straight to me
To help me win my war

I whisper your name over and over
My messages speed through the night
But you never hear me oh lover, dear lover
Perhaps I'm not doing it right

If it were possible for a dream
To call another dream
Then surely I'd get through
Can it be possible you've not heard
One solitary word
That's singing in the air
Or is it possible you don't care
The way I care
For you

Missed Understandings

Alas for our missed understandings
The way that we played hide and seek
Alas for our unhappy landings
The words that we never could speak

Perhaps I was much too demanding
And you not the straightest of men
Alas for our missed understandings
I wish we could do it again

I've learned how ambition can burn you
And battles can leave you with scars
I'd give all I've got to return to
Those missed understandings of ours

Black Song

I've seen the beauty of Barry's black eyes
Eyes of a mystic who's not very wise
Angel of death from some lost paradise
I'm haunted by Barry's black eyes

I've heard the beating of Barry's black heart
After he's practised his turbulent art
Watching him sleep as the darkness departs
I ponder on Barry's black heart

I've heard the beating of Barry's black wings
Hidden my eyes from the mischief he brings
Suffered the outrageous arrows and stings
To fly upon Barry's black wings

Wasted

Wasted are these days that I don't spend with you
Wasted are my empty nights
Wasted are these mornings and this postcard view
Wasted all the spring delights

Tasted once the happiness your love could bring
Tasted what your lips could do
Now the falling blossoms and the fireflies
Are wasted like my love for you

Wasted are these scenes that I don't share with you
Maytime melting into June
Pasted on the ceiling of this velvet night
Sequins, stars and silver moon

Wasted are the letters that I never send
Wasted are the poems I pen
Wasted my creations and my crazy dreams
Till I'm in your arms again

Motor Lullaby

I love the sound of cars
Sighing through my dreams
In semi-darkened rooms
After making love

I've heard their lullaby
On sultry summer nights
Beside some sleeping boy
After making love

Headlights splash their patterns
Like abstract moving pictures
Across so many ceilings
High and low
People sweeping onward
To different destinations
Have touched me in the darkness
As they go

The boys all fall asleep
And trap me in their arms
Outside the tyres sigh
Their motor lullaby

City Scapes

City Scapes

A Different Dream

I
The city is a different dream to everyone who comes
Some find the towers in the sky, some settle for the slums

From towns and villages we come on train and plane and bus
And will we storm the citadel or will it conquer us?

Anything can happen in the city
We meet the people that we may become
Advertisements flash seductive slogans
The in-crowd always drinks this brand of rum

The clothes, the jokes, the names to drop, you better get it right
Who's in, who's out, who's up, who's down, it changes overnight

The towers shine like dragon's teeth, the many treasures gleam
We brave the city's angry roar to dream a different dream

II
You're one more greenhorn searching for a style to make your own
You plot your overnight success and leap to get the phone

The people in the flat next door are loud with endless beers
You fall asleep alone at night Australians in your ears

In the city you can wear your dream life
Appear in any fantasy you choose
Satin gowns and gangster suits from Oxfam
Or bondage strides and correspondent shoes

We crowd together in the tube like rabbits in a hutch
But gurus and encounter groups must teach us how to touch

The prizes that are on display are seldom what they seem
But here at least we can be free to dream a different dream

Christmas Blues

The Christmas truce is over
It's really such a bore
We've eaten all the turkey
So now it's back to war
I don't know why you tarry
It all seems such a waste
And after Christmas pudding
You leave a bitter taste

I've got the Christmas blues, the Christmas blues
The kind you can't drown in an ocean of booze

We gave each other presents
We really tried to please
We filled the children's stockings
Hung tinsel on the trees
But after Christmas dinner
The brandy and the Queen
There's nothing to console us
Except the TV screen

I've got the Christmas blues *etc*

The Christmas tree is weeping
With candles all aglow
You never tried to kiss me
Beneath the mistletoe
Our revels now have ended
It's all gone awfully wrong
So join me in the singing
Of this bitter Christmas song

I've got the Christmas blues *etc*

Yankee Doodle Londoner
(with Craig Sams)

Well I've lived here in London town for fifteen long, wet years
And all my babes and buddies have become my mates and dears
I call my sweaters jumpers and I've learned to say *tomato*
Sometimes I try too hard and change potato *to potato*
Chorus: But I just cant say 'can't. No I just cant say *can't*
I'd do most anything you want but I just cant say *can't*

I used to know by A to Z now that's my A to Zed
My tongue is never twisted luv except when we're in bed
A platings what I give you now; it's head I used to serve
And now I bowl a leg-break where I used to pitch a curve
Chorus: But I just cant say *can't* etc

My washcloth is my flannel, my apartment is my flat
I saunter down to Soho and have dinner at the Trat
I know the drill, I've sussed the scene, it's biscuit now not cookie
I've got a turf accountant where I used to have a bookie
Chorus: But I just cant say *can't* etc

Smart trousers clothe my lower half; the men here don't wear pants
I go for dirty weekends but I don't say Paris France
I'm a Yankee Doodle Londoner as any chap can see
But there's one little word that gives the show away on me
Chorus: I simply cant say *can't* etc

I don't say balls, it's bollocks, wow! how English can you get
I've even learned to offer everyone a cigarette
But if there ever comes a day when I say *can't* for cant
My buddies from the States will think I'm just a gay transplant
Chorus: So I just cant say *can't* etc

One of Those Days

This morning we went to a screening
Half way people started to cough
In Soho at lunch we saw the old bunch
By three everyone drifted off
The film was a definite let down
Now what sort of game can we play?
We're jumpy but flat. Who's for kicking the cat?
No hope of redeeming the day

It's one of those days when you're ready for something
But nothing keeps coming along
The doorbell will ring but it's only Jehovah
And he's got the house number wrong

It's one of those days when you're ready and willing
To travel to heaven or hell
There's sun and there's rain and a sky full of thunder
Which makes you feel restless as well

Seeing a film in the daytime
Is often an awful mistake
Life is a bit disappointing
After you take a reality break

The dope that you're smoking has made a suggestion
But nothing turns into a song
It's one of those days when you're ready for something
But zilch is what's coming along
Sweet F.A. is coming along

Doner Kebabs

I've got the 'flu, my mate's got crabs
I pick my nose, he picks his scabs
And all our dreams are up for grabs
We blame it all on Doner Kebabs
Doner Kebabs, Doner Kebabs, *etc*

See that hunk of greyish yuck
Standing in the window of the local Greek
That's your meat? Well lots of luck
It lets you down, it leaves you weak

We blow our bread on dope and cabs
We can't afford to pay our tabs
There's just one thought that really stabs
Our downfall comes from Doner Kebabs,
Doner Kebabs, Doner Kebabs, *etc*

Who knows what they make it from
Danny's got a theory that it comes from Mars
It wastes your brain, it wrecks your bum
It turns you green, it maims, it scars

Doner Kebabs, Doner Kebabs
I've got the 'flu, my mate's got crabs
I pick my nose, he picks his scabs
We blame it all on Doner Kebabs

The Early Winds of Morning

In the early winds of morning
She hurries home to bed
And a hundred happy pictures
Are dancing in her head

As she races with her shadow
Chased by the rising sun
She feels guilty and delighted
And proud of what she's done

The early winds of morning are singing to her lover
He can see her in the mirror as he shaves
And his hand's a little shaky as he lives the long night over
And he wonders if it's true that Jesus saves

As she tiptoes down the hallway
She cringes at each creak
And her heart is beating loudly
Her knees are feeling weak

She slips in beside her husband
That boring, snoring heap
And the early winds of morning
Will send her off to sleep

London Days and New York Nights

My favourite cities are London and New York
Each has its unique delights
The perfect city would be a bit of both
London days and New York nights

London afternoons are smoke and laughter
London is a brave December rose
New York nights are like a roller coaster
New York has those bars that never close

New York is a man of steel with murder in his eyes
London is a lady, fair, cool and worldly wise
New York is amphetamine, London's charm and ease
New York grabs you by the heart, Londoners say "please"

London has the Palace and the Tower
New York has the Lady Liberty
New York has a reckless risky rhythm
Something sweet and salty from the sea

London in the afternoon is living in a dream
Soho pubs were Behan boozed, strawberries and cream
London treasures verbal grace, eccentricities
Ghosts of Shakespeare, Shaw and Wilde stroll beneath the trees

London and New York are my two lovers
Each has its traditions, toys and tunes
If you want to make me happy give me
New York nights and London afternoons

The Media and Me

The Media and Me

In Bed with a Book

They think I'm just a bit of fluff
And try to buy me minks
But I get bored with all that stuff
'Cause I'm a girl who thinks
I don't avoid encounters that are sexual
But I am basically an intellectual

I love to curl up in bed with a good book
Be it fact or fiction
'Cause nothing goes to your head like a good book
That is my conviction

Don't want to go out to theatres and nightclubs
When the nights are stormy
I love to cuddle in bed with some cocoa
And a book to warm me

I can have a ball with old Stendhal
With Hardy I am happy
When I'm in the hay with Hemingway
There's just no beating Pappy

But please don't think that I've missed all the wild life
'Cause I'm not a dead one
I love to curl up in bed with a good book
Or a friend who's read one

I can see things clear with Germaine Greer
Len Deighton keeps me guessing
I can get a bang from R.D. Laing
And bawl with Doris Lessing

Name any novel from Dickens to Mailer
And honey I can quote it
I love to curl up in bed with a good book
Or the chap who wrote it

New Wave Film
(or Everything Changes but the Avant-Garde)

"I'm bored," she says. Her eyes are bright red.
"Don't cry," he says, "try screaming instead."
"I'm twelve years old and already dead!"
"You're sick," he says, "let's get into bed."

Then cut to bed, the shape of a swan
She's wearing pearls with nothing else on
He stares ahead, unbuttons his shirt
"Come on," she says and throws him a skirt

Shot of news stand
Moving tram
Screaming headlines
Traffic jam

They writhe on bed. The music goes wild
"Good God," he says, "you're only a child."
A tank rolls in and one or two goats
Two small red wounds appear on his throat

Shots of Belsen
Mushroom cloud
Angry faces
In a crowd

We cut to her. She's eating a glass
"Get stuffed," he says, "I'm going to mass"
He falls down stairs with joy in his eyes

He's sure to cop a festival prize

The Bull Also Rises

A literary baritone was Ernest Hemingway
He beat upon his hairy chest to prove he wasn't gay
The good, the true, the perfect kill were what he most admired
The dying lion and the bull his manly prose inspired

F. Scott Fitzgerald wrote about the things girls do to boys
The dream that just exceeds our grasp and how we break our toys
He wrote in accents bitter-sweet about the idle rich
And Scott was just a sad young man but Ernest was a bitch

Ernest and Scott, Ernest and Scott
Ernest loved killing and Scotty did not
Publishers know that they're still pretty hot
So sells the story of Ernest and Scott

In Paris once upon a time they shared some fun and wine
When all the very best *bon mots* were made by Gertrude Stein
And everything was written down and still the memoirs pour
What Ernest said to Scott one day is now a dreadful bore

Ernest and Scott, Ernest and Scott
Scott died of drink and the Hollywood rot
Ernest showed death he could make the last shot
So ends the glory of Ernest and Scott
So sells the story of Ernest and Scott

Peter Lorre

Peter Lorre, small and stealthy
Slips through misty nights and morning
On his way to scenes of carnage

Peter Lorre, weak and wicked
Sneaking down some sordid alley
Sometimes whining, sometimes wistful

Because he has no power
He needs to creep and crawl
A weary weeping monster
His back is to the wall

Like a dissipated baby
Smoking with a hand that trembles
Sigh and sigh for Peter Lorre

Never fondled by a woman
He's so soft and sadly human
Say a prayer for Peter Lorre

Christopher Robin Where Are You?

Christopher Robin
Whatever happened to you?
Where is your Nanny
And Piglet and Winnie the Pooh?

Balding and paunchy
And sad in some semi-detached
Watching the tele
While outside the nightmares are hatched

The world your father made lives on
A never-ending summer
While crazy days of rock and rage
Roll on towards the ultimate bummer

Christopher Robin
Have you a son of your own?
Does he take Pooh Bear
To basements where people get stoned?

While you grow older
And full of the fears of today
Safe at the top of the forest
A boy and a bear always play

It Beats Watchin' Television

So glad to see you in my neighbourhood
When you're around I'm not so sad
'Cause when you're good you're very, very good
And when you're bad, you're not so bad

I confess that I'm a sucker
For this little game we play
It beats watchin' television anyway
And you know that I'll forgive you
If your fingers start to stray
It beats watchin' television anyway

You can tease me, you can squeeze me
And it's really quite OK
It's more fun than goin' fishin' anyway
And I hope that you've been peeping
Through my see-through negligée
It beats watchin' television anyway

It's better than walkin', better than talkin'
Better than singing the blues
Baby please ride me, when you're inside me
I can forget all that bad, bad news

When our bodies come together
Ain't we happy in the hay
It's more fun than modern dancing or ballet
Though it may not last for ever
There's one thing I want to say
It beats classes in ceramics anyway
And it beats watchin' television anyday!

The Lonesome Monster

The Creature from the Black Lagoon
He means the world no harm
He dreams the shapely scientist
Will take him in her arms
No female monster ever comes
In answer to his cries
And at the ending of the film
The monster always dies

Monsters get lonesome
Their lives are brutish, short and wet
Nights filled with longing
For eyes they've never met
Warm thighs they'll never get

Friends never call them
Men tend to greet them with a gun
When monsters drop in
They only eat and run
And spoil the children's fun

No one to hold them, no one to scold them
Nothing but hunger inside
No one to wake with, jump in the lake with
Nothing to hug but their pride

Poor, lonesome monster
Though he has muscles strong as steel
He's just a looser
He's got no sex appeal
To help him make a deal
Poor, insecure lonesome monster

Instant Nostalgia

Nostalgia graced the 30's and the 40's and the 50's
Now the big 60 revival's almost here
The periods are speeding up with shorter spaces leading up
Nostalgia's growing closer every year
Since we'll soon be running out of styles to borrow
Here's the trendy conversation of tomorrow

I remember this morning
As though it was yesterday
I was reading the paper
But the news got in the way

I remember the teapot
The orange juice fresh and cold
My egg was eggstatic
And the yellow shone like gold

Each object at breakfast stands out clearly
Though memory may lend a rosy glow
This evening we stare through misty windows
It seems such a stale and shoddy show
Remember the clothes we wore this morning
By lunchtime we'd thrown them all away
Remember the music of this morning
The pop songs of violence and decay

What a fabulous breakfast
I buttered the toast at dawn
It cannot be reheated
But the memory lingers on

Though the world has grown older
And there isn't much left to say
I remember this morning
As though it were yesterday